Praise for *Indian Giver*

"What impresses me most about John Smelcer, aside from his powerful writing, is his indomitable spirit."
— James Welch, author of *The Indian Lawyer* & *Fools Crow*

"When it comes to revisioning the Native American experience, few are as triumphant as John Smelcer."
— Howard Zinn, author of *A People's History of the United States*

"Replete with irony and wit, *Indian Giver* is an astute and intelligent exploration of what it means to be Native American in the 21st century."
—Maria Gillan, American Book Award winner

"There's an authority of landscape here—true grounding and not just the flippant acknowledgment of sources in so much contemporary poetry. I feel the primal grain and temper of the genuine here."
—William Heyen

"The very title of this strong, somber, and beautiful collection prepares the reader for the long familiar list of injustices practiced upon the Native Peoples of this continent, and for the fully justified bitterness and anger left behind by those injustices. This dark, unflinching book tells its own truth persuasively and starkly."
—Rhina Espaillat

"Angry, honest, proud. . . . The huge range of poems gathered here create a lament, a protest, and an inextinguishable song."
—Sherod Santos

"I would argue—and rightly so—that John Smelcer is among the best and most original poets in America."
—Stanley Kunitz, former Poet Laureate of the United States

"Nothing short of splendid. Like an alley fight fought on the petals of a rose."
—Robert Nazarene, author of *Margie*

"Smelcer's deceptively direct poems have the kind of energy found in the poems of William Carlos Williams and Gary Snyder. Worth hearing or reading again and again."
—Joseph Bruchac

Praise for *Without Reservation*

"Clear, rueful, courageous, sardonic, hard-lived. Poems with a sweet clarity that leaves us with no excuse. To be taken straight."
—Gary Snyder, original Beat and Pulitzer Prize winner

Praise for *Songs from an Outcast*

"John Smelcer's poems bring one a strong sense of his ancestry, his constant and haunting awareness of the indigenous life so grievously wounded yet still alive around and in him. This gives his work an unusual and valuable resonance."
—Denise Levertov

"John Smelcer is among the most brilliant younger poets in recent American literature."
—Allen Ginsberg

"This poet speaks from the land and for the land and for the people who belong to it."
—Ursula K. Le Guin

Indian Giver

Books by John Smelcer

Fiction

Stealing Indians
Savage Mountain
Edge of Nowhere
Lone Wolves
The Trap
The Great Death
Alaskan: Stories from the Great Land

Native Studies

The Raven and the Totem
A Cycle of Myths
In the Shadows of Mountains
The Day That Cries Forever
Durable Breath
Native American Classics
We are the Land, We are the Sea

Poetry

The Indian Prophet
Songs from an Outcast
Riversong
Without Reservation
Beautiful Words
Tracks
Raven Speaks
Changing Seasons

INDIAN GIVER

JOHN SMELCER

POEMS

FOREWORDS BY
RUTH STONE, DIANE WAKOSKI & X. J. KENNEDY
ILLUSTRATION BY R. CRUMB

Leapfrog Press
Fredonia, New York

Published in 2016 in the United States by
Leapfrog Press LLC
PO Box 505
Fredonia, NY 14063
www.leapfrogpress.com

Printed in the United States of America

Distributed in the United States by
Consortium Book Sales and Distribution
St. Paul, Minnesota 55114
www.cbsd.com

First Edition

Library of Congress Cataloging-in-Publication Data

Names: Smelcer, John E., 1963- author. | Crumb, R., illustrator.
Title: Indian giver / John Smelcer ; forewords by Ruth Stone, Diane Wakoski
& X. J. Kennedy ; illustration by R. Crumb.
Description: First edition. | Fredonia, New York : Leapfrog Press, 2016. |
St. Paul, Minnesota : Distributed in the United States by Consortium Book
Sales and Distribution
Identifiers: LCCN 2015036505 (print) | LCCN 2015041088 (ebook) | ISBN
9781935248804 (softcover : acid-free paper) | ISBN 9781935248811 (epub)
Subjects: | BISAC: POETRY / Native American. | POETRY / American / General.
Classification: LCC PS3569.M387 A6 2016 (print) | LCC PS3569.M387 (ebook) |
DDC 811/.54–dc23
LC record available at http://lccn.loc.gov/2015036505

811
5

for Howard Zinn

Acknowledgments

Poems in this collection first appeared in: *88: A Journal of Contemporary American Poetry, American Voice, Appalachia, Artful Dodge, Art Times, Asymptote, Bombay Gin, Clay Palm Review, Common Review, Contemporary Literary Horizons* (Bucharest), *Crossborders, Cumberland Poetry Review, Forma Fluens* (Italy), *Fox Cry Review, Free Press, Fugue, Generation X, Georgetown Review, Harpur Palate, Hawaii Pacific Review, Hayden's Ferry Review, International Poetry Review, Iowa Review, Iron Horse, Journal of Alaska Native Arts, Kenyon Review, Literary Matters, The Literary Review, Midwest Poetry Review, Modern Literature in Translation, Nimrod, Natural Bridge, North American Review, Oklahoma Review, Orbis* (UK), *Papyrus, Paterson Literary Review, Paradox, Pebble Lake Review, Pembroke, Pemmican, Poetry Ireland Review, Prairie Schooner, Puerto Del Sol, Ragazine, Raven Chronicles, Rosebud, Runes, Seventh Quarry* (Wales), *Verse Daily, Wisconsin Academy Review, Witness,* and *Yuan Yang* (UK).

This manuscript, originally entitled *American Indian Dreams,* was a finalist for the Crab Orchard Poetry Series Award from Southern Illinois University and the University of Wisconsin Poetry Series Award. "After a Sermon at the Church of Infinite Confusion" received Honorable Mention in the 2004 James Hearst Poetry Prize awarded by the *North American Review* and appeared in *Native American Classics* (2013). A version of "Road Map" received an Honorable Mention in the 2010 AWP College Writing Awards. "The Road to Chitina" and "Potlatch" appeared in *Here First: Autobiographical Essays by Native American Writers* (Eds. B. Swann and A. Krupat, 2000). "Durable Breath" appeared in *Durable Breath: Contemporary Native American Poetry* (1994). "The Book of Genesis, Revised for American Indian History" and "Indian Re-Education" appears in *Genocide in America* (Open University of Israel, 2009, renewed 2013). R.

Crumb illustration from *The Book of Genesis Illustrated* (W. W. Norton & Company, Inc. © 2009) used with permission.

The author thanks X. J. Kennedy, Ruth Stone, Diane Wakoski, R. Crumb, Mark Strand, James Welch, Seamus Heaney, Bard Young, Robert Nazarene, Stanley Kunitz, Maria Gillan, Catherine Creger, Aeronwy Thomas, Joe Weil, Aaron Fine, Amber Johnson, Jenny Marcus, Roxanne Dunbar-Ortiz, Joseph Bruchac, and Lisa Graziano.

The Great Spirit gave this land to us.
Then he took it away
and gave it to someone else. Indian Giver.

"The conquest of the earth,
which mostly means the taking it away
from those who have a different complexion
or slightly different noses than ourselves,
is not a pretty thing when you look into it too much."
—Joseph Conrad, *Heart of Darkness*

"History is not history unless it is the truth."
—Abraham Lincoln

Contents

Intermission

Forewords

Daring, brilliant, and absolutely defiant! In a world where such poets are more rare than people might imagine, John Smelcer is one of the truly great poets I have come across in my life. His poetry is of genius, and in his country of snow, glaciers, and the inevitable loss of languages and traditions, each poem rides, as Robert Frost expressed it, on its own slow melting. In so doing, these poems are honest, exquisite, sad, funny, and beautiful, beautiful, beautiful. I am thrilled that this collection will bring people into further awareness of such an extraordinary poet and the unworried being of his heart-melting poems.

—Ruth Stone, winner of the National Book Award and the National Book Critic's Circle Award

I wrote my original foreword to this book more than a decade ago. But over the years, the manuscript has evolved to the point it deserves a new foreword. In the earlier version I wrote that "while the poet has a bit of a chip on his shoulder about the miseries he has inherited, he also is a good man, one who is trying to solve and understand the problems from the past." In this new *Indian Giver,* this anger is more focused into an irony that shapes the book, as when Smelcer responds in "Skins" to another Native writer, one who has sold out his integrity of tradition:

"Bigshot Indian-writer tells me to stop writing about Indian stuff, says none of the true skins will have anything to do with me."

Smelcer then contrasts their city-slick lives with his own before he walks home,

in the dark
to my little cabin on the bluff above the river,
shake out my clogged dreamcatcher,
and sit looking out the window
wondering what the hell I'm supposed to write about.

This more muted shaping of the anger and feelings of
hopelessness that a well-educated traditionalist feels, turns
this book into a dynamic drama. Smelcer's biography allows
the reader to see to what lengths an angry but non-violent
man can go to, learning several Native languages, writing
dictionaries and books that keep them from going extinct
and writing, writing, always telling stories, keeping the fish
being smoked by the river alive alongside the ironies of sur-
vivors. His opening poem, "The Book of Genesis, Revised
for American Indian History" is a gorgeous piece of rheto-
ric, a great read-aloud poem which begins:

and then one day God created Indians
and he saw that they were good
and he loved them for a really long time,
but then he got mad at them
because they didn't speak English or something. . . .

Even though Smelcer has a page full of credits and pub-
lications, he is not a rarified writer. He is clearly writing
in Whitman's tradition, speaking the language of the com-
mon people. He sings to the cosmos, as Whitman might say.
And his words are simple, good. They bring light.
—Diane Wakoski, author of *Emerald Ice*

You won't meet another book like *Indian Giver* this year, nor in any year. To paraphrase Walt Whitman, who touches this book touches an entire people, not only a man. Starting with its title, it abounds in bitter humor. Reading it, I often felt torn between an impulse to laugh and a painful sense of compassion—which is how I respond to the greatest literature, from *King Lear* to *War and Peace*.

Among our leading writers, John Smelcer is unique: novelist and poet, scholar and linguist and social commentator. An enrolled member of the Ahtna tribe, he sees the Native American from both outside and inside, giving him the rare insights so forthrightly expressed in these memorable poems. Smelcer beautifully demonstrates the stupidity of hate, and in vivid profiles of individuals shows the rampant injustice that still afflicts them, as in the case of Willie Tensleep, who has half of his lottery winnings seized for taxes and the other half seized for the "Indian Tax," so that he stays poor. I'm amazed that so angry a book can be so sharp of eye and can bestow such pleasure. It's probably futile to try to introduce *Indian Giver* when far and away the most satisfactory introduction is to turn to page one and begin to read.

—X. J. Kennedy, editor of *LITERATURE,*
An Introduction to Poetry, An Introduction to Fiction,
and *The Bedford Reader*

The Book of Genesis,
Revised for American Indian History

In the beginning,
after forming the earth from the void
God said, "Let there be light"
and so there was

And God saw that this was good
so he divided light from darkness
and water from land;
and then one day God created Indians
and he saw that they were good
and he loved them for a really long time,
but then he must have got mad at them
because they didn't speak English or something
so he whispered in the ear of Christopher Columbus
to show the way for White people
who came to claim the land for themselves,
and God said unto them,

"From this day on you shall have dominion over Indians,"
which was kind of the same thing he told Adam
about the animals that creeped and crawled

and so it was
and so it was
and so it was

And God saw that this was good
so when he returned from a paid vacation in Rome
God said, "Let Indians be slaves to the Whites"
and so they were the first slaves to toil in the New World
but then the Whites ran out of Indians
so they imported Black people from far away
and that is all that people would remember
forever and ever, amen

And God knew that this was good
so he told White people to go west and multiply
and he said unto them,
"Let there be colonization,"
and so there was
and from his words sprang colonialism

who begat expansionism
who begat broken treaties
who begat assimilation
who begat disease
who begat wars
who begat genocide

Then one day after he made the dodo extinct
God decided that Indians needed exercise
so he created The Trail of Tears
and then he told the Whites to kill all the buffalo

so that Indians would become vegetarians

and so it was
and so it was
and so it was

After he got over a bad cold or something
God looked around and saw that Whites
were like locusts and they needed more land
to build condos and housing developments,
gas stations and convenience stores,
shopping malls and parking lots,
so he said, "Let there be reservations"
and lo they came into being
and from his words sprang dislocation

who begat racism
who begat poverty
who begat alcoholism
who begat depression
who begat suicide
who begat genocide

And God knew that this was good
so he created the Bureau of Indian Affairs
and land allotments and unscrupulous land embezzlers
and boarding schools where Indian children
were taught to forget what it means to be Indian,
then he created HUD Housing and commodity cheese,
rez dogs and bingo halls, casinos and
The Church of Infinite Confusion

And on the last day God returned from Wal-Mart
and the Mega-Mall and the cineplex
and he saw that Indians were no more upon the land

and he knew that this was a good thing
so he created the Lazy Boy and the remote control
and TV westerns and pay-per-view
and the Washington Redskins and the Cleveland Indians,
and from his comfortable reclining throne
God looked out across the land he had created
and he saw that it was good
and he called it America which means
"Place where Indians once roamed"

and so it was
and so it was
and so it was

After a Sermon at the
Church of Infinite Confusion

At ten, Mary Caught-in-Between
came home from sunday school,
told every animal and bird and fish
they couldn't talk anymore,
told her drum it couldn't sing anymore,
told her feet they couldn't dance anymore,
told her words they weren't words anymore,
told Raven and Coyote they weren't gods anymore,
said god was a starving white man
with long hair and blue eyes and a beard
who no one loved enough to save
when they nailed him to a totem pole.

The Incomplete & Unauthorized Definition of American Indian Literature

"Indian" is not a derogatory word.
It's what we call ourselves. We claim it.

Not all Indians wear long black hair
or faded red bandanas.

I've never seen a Red Man.

Percentage of people who say they are part Cherokee: 50

Percentage who claim to have a nameless great-grandmother
who was a Cherokee princess: 100

Percentage of actual Cherokee princesses in history: 0

Percentage of the Cherokee Nation compared to the number of all other recognized tribes in America: 0.2

Percentage of Americans who are enrolled Indians according to the U.S. Census Bureau: 0.67

Fiction by Indians outsells poetry by Indians,
yet poetry is the language of sorrow and heartbreak.

All Indians speak poetry,
yet no Indian has won the Pulitzer Prize for poetry.

This is the mathematical formula for deciphering
meaning in Native American poetry:

Where *a* represents *anger* and *s* represents *sorrow,*

let *P* represent *poetry* and *t* represent the duration
(*time*) of marginalization (expressed in centuries)

Thus, $P = t(a + s)^2$

Indian writers shouldn't drive sports cars.
I traded my yellow Porsche for a pick-up truck
with a quarter million miles
and a rifle rack in the rear window.

Not all Indians come from Horse Cultures.
Not all Indians ride horses.
I've only been on a horse once and it threw me.

Writing by Indians should contain dogs.
Many Indian writers have had at least
one of their dogs run over by a pick-up truck
with a rifle hanging in the rear window.

History is written by the victors.
Indians didn't always lose the battles.
Don't believe everything you've ever read
or watched on television.

John Wayne's real name was Marion, but directors figured
Marion the Cowboy couldn't believably defeat Indians.

Columbus didn't really discover America
the way you think he did.

The Navajo Nation is as big as Nebraska.

Bingo is Indian Social Security.

Federal enrollment is how the government

counts Indians to predict when we will become extinct.
Not all Indians are enrolled. I am enrolled.

Enrollment doesn't mean anything.

There are 500 tribes in America. No individual speaks
for all of them, barely even for a single clan or tribe.

Some bigshot Indian writers think they speak for everyone.

Does an illiterate white shoe salesman in Idaho speak for
you?

American universities teach American Indian literature
but hire almost no Indian writers at all.
White professors who have never seen a reservation
teach American Indian literature
even when there's an Indian writer on faculty
because it's trendy.

Some Indians go to tribal colleges
Where they are taught by white teachers
who want to be Indian. New-Age white women
have sex with Indian men so they can become Indian.

You can't become Indian by proximity.

America loves the Indian-sounding names of places,
but they don't want Indians to live there.
It gives them a sense of connection to a land
upon which they have little history of their own.

Sometimes a sweat lodge is just a sweat lodge.

Some American sports teams are named for Indians.

There should be an Indian baseball team called
the Cherokee Crucified Christs, complete with
a bleeding team mascot nailed to a wooden cross.

Would that hurt your sensibilities?

All Indians aren't proud and defiant.

When I do something right, my Indian uncle
tells me I've earned an eagle feather.

Only Indians can own eagle feathers.

Nearly all published Indian writing is in English.
Almost no Indian writer speaks their Indian language.
Fewer yet can write in it.

Sii cetsiin koht'aene kenaege', tsin'aen.

Indian children love to dance Indian-style
but they don't understand a word the elders sing.

Indian boys love to beat Indian drums
while Indian girls sway in moving circles.

The hearts of Indian boys are tight-stretched drums.
The hearts of Indian girls are beautiful sad songs.

The government decimated bison
so that Indians would become vegetarians.

The government killed wild horses
so that Indian spirits would break.

The government sent Indian children to boarding schools

so they would forget being Indian. Missionaries built
The Church of Infinite Confusion so Indians would
forget being Indian.

I forget what I was trying to say.

British writers don't have to write about Shakespeare.
French writers don't have to write about Baudelaire.
Blacks don't always have to write about slavery.

Indian writers don't have to write about being Indian
or about dogs killed by trucks with gun racks
on reservations while fancy dancing,
wearing eagle feathers, and beating drums
while mouthing words to songs they do not know.

Many urban Indians write about life on the reservation
even when they've never lived on one because it sells better
than writing about going to Starbucks after shopping at the
Gap.

Few Indians have Indian-sounding names.
Non-Indians pretending to be Indians
 adopt names like "Runs-Beside-Spotted-Ponies,"
"Walks-With-Wolves," or "Deer Cloud."

A publisher once asked me to change my name
to a hyphenated one with a preposition and a spirit animal.

I replied, "How about Johnny Fakes-His-Name-on-a-Weasel?"

Audiences at readings by Indians are almost always white.

All Indian writers aren't spiritually attuned to Nature.
Most are fearful of getting lost in the woods.

Some Indians write out of anger and despair.
All Indian writers aren't angry and depressed.

Native America is drowning in a sea of alcohol.
Indians commit suicide ten times more often than whites.
Day after day, our hearts are turned into cemeteries.

The impoverished state of our lives is not self-inflicted.

Most Indian writers are mixed-blood
who hate the term "Half-Breed."

I am the son of a half-breed father.

I am an outcast. Even my shadow
tries to hide its face in shame

Deer on a Snowy Field

When the soldiers come
they start shooting
everyone—women
and the very old,
even our children.
I see them toss babes
into the air for target practice.

We run across a snowy field.

Soldiers on horseback mow us down
with swords and pistols or trample us.

I grab my granddaughter,
clutch her to my chest,
run for a creek bed—
screams and gunshots
and hoof beats behind us.

I pray that we turn into deer.

I run as fast as my old bones
can carry me, and I think,
"This is crazy.
I can't outrun
bullets and horses.
I'm too old to save anyone."

But I run anyway,
barefoot in the snow,
carrying the girl, chanting
"Deer, deer. Be a deer."

My granddaughter,
who sees them gaining
over my shoulder,
whispers in my ear,

"I believe in you, Grandmother.

I believe."

What the Old Man Said

My children, what they say is true.

They killed my whole tribe,
everyone but me.

They tossed infants into the air
for shooting practice.

They set the world afire;
even the stars burned.

My children, when you see them coming,
run away and don't look back.

Keep running.
Keep running.

Run.

An American Indian
Dreams the American Dream

Silas Carries-a-Dream sat on his porch
reading newspaper want ads looking for a job

He imagined what it would be like

        to go to work
        to wear a suit and tie
        new shoes
        carry a brief case
        punch a clock
        sit in a cubicle
        have a portfolio
        stock options
        take power lunches
        drink martinis
        get an ulcer
        get depressed

and jump from the twenty-seventh floor
on a Monday morning

When he was done
Silas crumpled the paper into a fist
and sent it rolling across the desert
like a tumbleweed

Dream Walker

Silas Carries-a-Dream was spinning
the hoop of his young dreams with a stick
along a crumbled edge of highway—

heat waves melting the uncertain road ahead.

It was a good dream as dreams go.

He was rolling his dreams

                rolling his dreams

toward a dark and crumbling horizon.

Kite Runners

Marty and Luther Sitting Bear
build kites from broken boughs of a piñon tree
cover them with pieces of cloth
cut from their grandmother's old Sunday dress,
make tails out of red, white, and blue bandanas
then run as fast as they can into the desert wind—

their hopeful dreams flying

on and on and on
on and on and on

How to Make Blue Ribbon
Indian Fry Bread

"Indians could spend their whole lives
looking for the perfect piece of fry bread."
——Sherman Alexie, *Reservation Blues*

In a large bowl, mix the following ingredients:

Three cups of flour made from the ashes
of failed Indian dreams

One cup of water made from the tears of Indian mothers

A pinch of salt, first thrown into open wounds
of Indian fathers

Drop the rolled and molded dough into a pan of oil
hot enough to incinerate every Indian future

Remove when both sides turn brown and blistered

The Alternate History of
the United States of America

Lester Has-Some-Books builds a time machine
in his uncle's garage and sets it to the day
Columbus discovers America.

Quickly, with the masts of three ships
lurching on the horizon, he sets up a big sign
on the beach:

WELCOME TO SPAIN!

Columbus spies the sign from the bay,
scratches his head, and orders all three ships
to turn around and head back out to sea.

Thing You Didn't Know About
American History #138

for Howard Zinn

Shortly after an adulterous winter of wife-swapping,
and after murdering a neighboring Indian tribe
in cold blood—

every man, woman, and child
while asleep in their beds—

the Pilgrims outlawed Christmas for decades,
making it illegal to celebrate the birth of Christ.

So much for America being founded on religious principles

Template for Treaties Between the United States of America and Indian Tribes

{U.S. GPO Document 7342-1; 1868-Rev.}

By the authority pursuant to US §100-10, an Act of Congress, this is a Treaty between the United States of America and the {name of Indian tribe goes here}, a legally binding instrument, duly signed, and witnessed by Authorized Signatories of the United States and the aforementioned tribe, hereinafter referred to as "Sucker."

In exchange for, and in consideration of, goods received {list of trinkets and trifles goes here}, the United States forthwith steals (hereafter referred to as "Purchases") the following land {vague description of land goes here} *ad valorem.* Upon execution, Sucker agrees to forfeit all rights and claims to aforesaid Purchase in perpetuity and to indemnify and hold harmless the United States.

This agreement, entered into with good faith and in consideration that Indians are unable to read the contents herein with its jargon and non sequiturs, is subject to amendment or termination without notice or restitution by the second-signing party, for which the first-signing party forfeits all rights or provisions for future redress, retribution, or adjudication in a U.S. Court of Law.

IN WITNESS WHEREOF the Parties hereto have executed this Treaty on this ___ day of _____, *anno domini* 18___, in accordance to the privileges and God-given mandate of manifest destiny of these United States of America, *quid pro quo, carpe diem, deus ex machina, caveat venditor, tempus fugit, mundus ex nihilo, magna cum laude, e pluribus unum, in excelsis deo, tu es perfututum.*

[Authorized Signatories of Indian Tribe goes here]

[Authorized Signatories of United States of America goes here]

Duke Sky Thunder Tries a Jedi Mind Trick on Non-Native America

This isn't the land you were looking for.

Move along.

If Charlie Brown Had Been
Set on a Reservation

Lucy would work for the Bureau of Indian Affairs.
With a big leering grin she'd promise Charlie Brown
that she wouldn't break the treaty *this* time
if only he'd sign on the bottom line.

"Don't you trust me, Charlie Brown?" she'd taunt.

And wouldn't you know that fool would fall for it every time.

Indian Superheroes

Chuck Norris and Billy Jack team up to fight injustice
on every reservation. Wearing boot-cut blue jeans,
faded denim jackets, and black hats with eagle feathers
tucked in the beaded bands they:

> karate chop unemployment & poverty
> sucker punch alcoholism & Fetal Alcohol Syndrome
> side kick obesity & diabetes
> head butt depression & suicide
> knee groin lack of educational opportunity
> Judo flip substandard housing & medical care
> hammer fist disillusion
> > and put hopelessness in a headlock.

With a big grin Billy Jack says to bigotry,
"I'm gonna put *this* foot against *that* side of your head,"

while Chuck Norris waggles his little pinkie finger
and domestic violence unclenches its angry fists
and flees in fear.

The Last Fancy Dancer

Clarence Hoop Dancer cried red tears
the night the last song man died.
There will be no more songs
around the everlasting fire,
no more young men
to leap and dance like flames.

No more drums.
No more dancers.

He stood outside and cried
beneath the stars, the stars,
flowers of his country.

The Day the Words Died

On the day their language died
the people gathered unspoken words

in buckets and brown paper bags
in suitcases and cardboard boxes

tossed those ghosts of words
onto a great funeral pyre

and, one by one, flung themselves
into the dreadful fire.

What the Medicine Man Said

You are sick. . . . Inside.
Here, he said, touching my heart.
Their world has destroyed your spirit,
deprived you of meaning and pride,
tells you that you must want the wrong things,
things that only reinforce emptiness.

You need powerful medicine—
        Indian medicine.

Sit down.
I will tell you a story.

Transfiguration Sunday

Easter Sunday, 1928. Father Slooko
stands before the Eucharist,
his face and hands raised to Heaven
as he recites The Last Supper.

"And after pouring wine into the cups of his disciples,
Jesus said,
Drink this, all of you, for this is the headwaters of my blood.
Then, he took out a salmon from a basket, held it up,
and said,
Eat this, all of you, for this is my body, which is given up unto you."

After Mass, the congregation streams out the double doors,
wades into the river, turns into a school of salmon,
and swims out to sea.

Indians are like salmon—at one time or another
they all leave the village or reservation,
only to come home when it's time to die.

The Ballad of Victor ComesAlong

Jesus was giving a sermon on the mount
when he noticed it was time for supper.
He looked around and saw he had no food
          to feed the multitude.

Just then, Victor ComesAlong passed by
with a huge sack of fry bread slung over his shoulder.
Victor gave his sack of bread to Jesus, who blessed him.

From that day on everyone called it a miracle.

Literary Criticism

Catherine Has-Some-Books sat on a rock
talking to Johnny Looks-Too-White about Shakespeare.

"Hamlet must have been Indian," she said,
"because everyone was out to get him."

"Romeo must have been Indian," he said,
"because white folks never let their daughters marry Indians."

"Lear must have been Indian," they nodded,
"because he lost everything in the end."

They held each other as the sun abandoned the reservation,
certain that Shakespeare must have been Indian.

The Party Crashers

after a poem by Glen Simpson

Federal agents in black suits and black SUVs
crashed the Indian powwow.

The Man from the government said:

You gotta have a permit from the state

>   To assemble as Indians
>   To dance as Indians
>   To drum as Indians
>   To sing as Indians
>
>   To be Indians

Politically Incorrect

for Vincent Cache Smelcer (1978-2014)

My uncles and cousins sitting around a campfire.

A wolf howls on the dark mountain.
We all get up and dance and sing around the fire.

Huh ha! Hey! Hey! Huh ha!

Afterwards, one of my cousins says,
"Man, it's great to be Native American!"

My uncle slaps him upside the head
and all us Indians laugh for a long time.

Hymn Singer

At grandmother's funeral
I watch my Indian father
mouth words to "Amazing Grace"

> *Ts'in aen ne'k'eltaeni*
> *Ts'in aen ne'k'eltaeni*

and I am a stranger
dressed in something black.

Indian Policy

based on a true story

Silas Carries-a-Dream wanted to go to college
so he went to McDonalds™ to ask for a scholarship
but they said they only gave money to
African Americans, Asian Americans,
Hispanic Americans, Anyone-else-but-you-Americans,
because Indians are all rich from casinos and bingo.

So Silas went home to his pick-up truck camper on blocks,
sat at his rickety table beneath a cupboard of one dusty can,
took stock of all his worldly possessions:

> his Buick hubcap plate and bent fork
> one thin red blanket
> the leaky roof and broken window
> old issues of *Better Homes & Gardens*
> and his B&W television set
> with its skeletal umbrella antennae
> which only picked up westerns
> when it didn't rain.

He looked around, ashamed at his great display of wealth.

Indian Blues

Thomas Two Fists
whittled a guitar from a tree
that had fallen during a storm
and killed a shaman. He carved
the tuning pegs from the bones
of a white buffalo.
For strings,
he used the long gray hair of
old Indian mothers who had lost
their children and grandchildren
to alcohol and drunk driving.
For years,
Two Fists travelled from
reservation to reservation
and powwow to powwow
singing the blues.
Wherever he went,
Indians wrapped themselves in old blankets,

dreamed of forgotten homes and wept
dreamed of forgotten homes and wept.

Reservation Blues

All summer tourists pass
our village on the buckled highway

of this place seldom visited
where hearts slowly

do nothing but break,
where old Indian women and men

sell beadwork and dreamcatchers,
their pride so distant

it is carried only in memory
or forgotten in the blood,

and where I stand at the water's edge,
my clenched fists wide as the river.

The Road to Chitina

"It is not good to be poor,
and there are no coins in the wind."
                    —John Haines

From a weathered couch near the edge of a road
Indian men drink beer and count cars passing,

while inside a poor house of inconvenience
hungry children wait for their mother

sleeping off last night's binge on the
uncomfortable seat of an old truck.

Some are born amid surroundings
where things are not as simple as they seem.

In this place of interminable despair,
even the wind, with its faint scent of poverty,

hurriedly blows through the stirring village
then out across the wide floodplain.

Cowboys & Indians #1

All the children in our neighborhood
played Cowboys and Indians.

Of course, Indians always lost,
their women and horses taken,
and their teepees and blankets burned.

It's a good thing my Indian father
never saw me playing, always
dressed as a cowboy in a five-gallon hat
with two chrome six-guns and a silvery badge.

The Birthday Party

After the song was sung
candles extinguished
cake and ice cream consumed
and every present opened
the guests went outside to play
Cowboys & Indians

Indians hid behind trees and hedges
while cowboys rounded them up
and after shooting half
banished the rest to a condemned lot
on the poor side of town

Road Map

After dropping out of high school in the tenth grade
followed by years of unemployment, two failed marriages,
and falling off the wagon more times than he can remember,
Melvin Standing Still wonders where the hell he went wrong.

So he pulls out the tattered map of his life
carefully unhinges the torn and ragged folds
presses it flat on a table with both hands like an iron
leans over and traces its topography with a finger
frantically searching for the familiar X that says

You Are Here

Riversong

Tazlina Village, Alaska

I never want to leave this land.
All of my ancestors are buried here

listening to riversong
from picket-fenced graves—

their wind-borne spirits
linking past and present:

sii xu'ane tsiye, Tezdlende Joe
my great-grandfather, Tazlina Joe,

sii tsucde 'ł tsude, Ełdayudesnaa
my grandmother and her sister, Morrie Secondchief.

When I finally fall to pieces
this is where my pieces will fall.

An Indian Poet Apologizes
for His Color

Johnny Looks-Too-White ponders which
ethnicity box to check on a job application

I'm one-quarter Indian,
three-fourths White—
three times more White than Indian.
Half a half-breed. Less than nothing.

I don't fit in here or there.

Which parts of me are Indian?
Is it a molar, an earlobe, both thumbs,
my left testicle, the pinky toes?
Does it exist in that part of my heart
that only knows sorrow and loss,
or in my lungs, my duodenum,
every fourth blood cell?

I don't know if I should drum and dance
and sing to the mountains,

or go shopping at The Gap
after an espresso at Starbucks.

Dreamcatcher

I used to have a dog named Jesus.

Every night before bedtime
he'd go out back
and bury my bad dreams
in shallow graves
like old soup bones.

After thirteen years,
he died and the dreams returned.

I haven't had a good night's sleep since.

The Abandoned First Draft of the Preamble of the United States Constitution

We the ~~White~~ People of the United States, in Order to form a more perfect~~ly~~ ~~homogeneous~~ Union, establish ~~arbitrary~~ justice, insure domestic tranquility ~~for ourselves~~, provide for the common defense ~~of White settlements and their economic interests~~, promote the general welfare ~~by stealing all the land we see~~, and secure the Blessings of Liberty to ~~all White People~~ our Posterity, do ordain and establish this Constitution for the United States of America ~~subject to interpretation and excluding by law any persons of color~~.

This Is Just to Say

after a poem by William Carlos Williams

a note tacked to a tree in Indian country

we have
torn up the treaties
you signed
only yesterday

which you
paid for
in blood

We're sorry
but we need
your land
so green, so green

Telling the News

"Although the Indians won the battle,
they subsequently lost the war. . . ."
—from a National Park Service pamphlet

At Little Bighorn
the spirit of a warrior
asks me if they won the war
and I answer,

"Yes, my friend.
You won. You won."

Then the spirit of a soldier
asks me if they won the war
and I answer,

"Yes, my friend.
You won everything, everything."

Indian Time Machine

Lester Has-Some-Books
invents a time machine in his sweat lodge.

So, he sets it back to Little Bighorn
with a video camera and tapes everything.

Then he invites the whole damn reservation to watch
the movie. Everyone's eating popcorn and laughing.

It's really something. You should see it.
Everything's in color and there are these close-ups.

Here's the part where Custer sends in the cavalry
catching the Indians off guard.

Oh, and here's where three thousand Indians
chase them up a hill and whups their ass.

Betrayal

Judas Points-Him-Out
was one of the Crow scouts
that led Custer's 7th Cavalry
to the Indian encampment
at Little Bighorn.

He was paid thirty silver dollars.

With a name like that
seems like someone
should have seen it coming.

If Evel Knievel Were Indian

he would jump twenty-three semi-trailers
full of government commodity cheese
in a souped-up Indian motorcycle painted red.

He would line up every white guy who ever
played an Indian in a John Wayne western
and jump them all with his eyes closed
while twirling a sparkler in one hand.

If Evel Knievel were Indian
he would start at the moon
and pick up enough speed to soar
over every reservation—

a red and chrome meteor with its tires aflame.

Cowboys & Indians #2

*—at a steakhouse outside Missoula, Montana
with James Welch*

Silas Redcorn walked into a steak house
in the middle of cowboy country
wearing cowboy boots and a tee-shirt
with *Indian Pride* embroidered on the front.

While he waited for a waitress
who ignored his existence
all them cowboys glared at him
from beneath wide-brimmed hats

    black as storm clouds,

their sharp tongues coiled like barbed wire.

The Triumphant Conversion
of Mary Caught-in-Between

For many years, priests

at The Church of Infinite Confusion
tried to put the Fear of God
into little Mary Caught-in-Between.

It must have worked.

Come Sunday, she was always terrified
to walk through the chapel doors.

Our Lady of Sorrows

Every Sunday during Mass
Joseph Little Bear scrubbed the floors
and toilets of Our Lady of Sorrows
until his palms bled and no one
helped him to drag *his* cross

Fahrenheit

Sally Two Trees stood outside as the first snowflakes of winter

      began
                       to   fall.

She tried to catch them in her hands and on her tongue—
               each one a dream:

     a good job
     a nice home
     a college degree
     a car that didn't burn oil
     sobriety for her and her baby.

But every time Sally reached out to grasp one
the dream melted in her hand.

The Dead Are Lonely

Ever since Victor Lone Fight killed himself
with the sharp edge of a poem
all that remains of him is gray ash
spread across the reservation

on its dusty roads
in the dough of fry bread
in the braids of Indian women
in the ribcages of dead dogs

Intermission

We now interrupt your poetry reading pleasure
to debunk the myth of George Washington
as the stalwart archetype of American morality.

(Warning! This poem is dangerous.)

"You are hereby ordered to lay waste all [Indian] settlements . . .
so that the country may not be merely overrun but destroyed.
You will by no means listen to any pleas for peace
before you destroy their settlements. The Indians must see
that there is so much hatred in our hearts to destroy everything
that supports their very existence."

—Letter from Gen. George Washington to Major Gen. John
    Sullivan, 1775

Boarding School Arithmetic

At Wekonvertum Boarding School for Indian Eradication
we are taught how to add, subtract, multiply, and divide.

I learn quickly, faster than the others.

I count all the other children condemned to this school,
multiply it by the number of schools they tell us exist
across America, subtract that number from the set of all
Indian families, divide that by sorrow . . . squared,

and I realize that the future of Indians is zero.

A Wicked Irony

Mary Caught-in-Between was whipped
one hundred twenty-three times
at Wekonvertum Boarding School
for speaking Navajo during Latin—

a language dead for over a thousand years.

Problem Child

after a poem by Robert Conley

In her many years at
Wekonvertum Boarding School
Catherine Has-Some-Books
ran away twenty-seven times.

Whenever those
white teachers
were close
to finding her
she turned
into a doe
or a mouse
or a bird

and they never caught her

and they never understood.

An Indian Boy Dreams
of Being Billy Mills

After his very first day
at george armstrong custer elementary
Arthur Greased-Lightning
ran away from the BIA school
across its BIA playground
with its BIA swing hanging by one chain
and its BIA slide with no ladder
past neat rows of BIA houses
and his own BIA house
where his BIA brothers and sisters
sat on their BIA porch
past The First Baptist Church
of Indian Conversion
over Charlie Going-Nowhere
sleeping outside the bingo hall
beyond the Church of Infinite Confusion
and out across the wide plains
where he turned into a buffalo
then a coyote and a deer
and finally into tall prairie grass
racing in the wind

Durable Breath

Outside my cabin window,
I hear Raven's muffled caw rise from the river.

I think often of that night in your trailer at Nikiski,
of the old stories you told me, *Dena'ina Suk'dua,*
"That which is written on the people's tongues."

As a child you were beaten with a stick for speaking
your Native tongue. My father, born at Indian River,
does not know his mother's language. Tonight,

Kenaitze Indians gather at a Russian Orthodox church
to mourn in altered syllables among white-washed
crosses and tarnished silver icons. As I lean toward darkness,

it is your voice that lifts Raven's wings above the riverbank,
his ancient syllables rising like an ochre tide.

Call of the Wild

Once, I was a wolf
living among wolves

on the stunted backbone
of tundra and forests

where we hunted moose
and caribou all winter

in deep, drifted snow
without escape,

where only the expansive silence
of the far north listened

as we howled at the moon
and ran the glacial earth

until I awoke again a man.
Many years have passed,

but on some still nights
I hear them waiting

above the rim of this valley,
calling to me from shadows

like a visitor who comes to my home
and knocks on the door with both fists.

Returning the Gift

All summer, I have been feeding a raven
who comes to the river asking for salmon.

For weeks, we talk of the origin of things
while I cut fish to dry on racks in the sun.

Months later, when geese fly overhead
in long, slow arrows, I am lost moose hunting.

When night falls upon its dark knees and the moon
is a fingernail at the rim of the world,

I listen to tight-stringed wind
from inside my fluttering tent, and by morning,

in a shudder the world is wintered.
Quietly, through the stark white of the North,

I watch him arrive to lead me from the forest,
tree by tree, until I am home and we spoke for the last time.

Tsin'aen, Saghani Ggaay. Tsin'aen.
"Thank you, Great Raven. Thank you."

As he flies away towards far ochre mountains,
I hear him singing and singing.

A Polar Bear Prays for Colder Days Ahead

The world is melting beneath us.

Every year the ice pack shrinks, and we have to swim
farther and farther to fill our bellies.

We are not fish. We need the respite. Besides, on the ice
we catch seals and the occasional walrus—

even they need a place to hoist their weary bulk from the sea.
To quiet our raging hunger, we ramble inland, root

on the tundra, competing with wolves and grizzlies for caribou.
It is no easy thing to lose a world.

American Dreams

After watching a TV marathon
of *Leave it to Beaver*
and *The Andy Griffith Show*,
William Keeps-the-Fire went outside
to watch his reservation:
saw children playing
in abandoned trucks and refrigerators
rotting in fields,
cast stones at hungry dogs
tearing open garbage bags
when he walked past rows
of subsidized housing
where poverty settled on everything
like fine, red dust.

That night William Keeps-the-Fire dreamed
black-and-white dreams of a faraway heaven.

Indian Scalper

Jessie BlackHawk
standing in the rain
outside a stadium
illegally selling tickets
to a Redskins game

Indian Re-Education

The Dawes Act of 1887 tried to force
farming initiatives upon American Indians

After a hundred generations of hunting bison
Elijah High Horse turns a rocky field with a plow
where nothing grows in the garden, only sorrow,
and curses the gods who made stones.

Willie Tensleep Wins the Lottery

Willie TenSleep won the lottery
and after losing half to state and federal taxes
men in black suits with brief cases
came and said he had to pay the Indian Tax
which claimed the other half
because it's policy to keep Indians poor.

They left poor Willie standing
in a cloud of dust on a thirsty road
clutching the empty purse of his shadow

        searing into sand.

Fish Camp

Oscar Gray Wolf hid behind some bushes
watching Birdie Yazzie crouched beside the river
cutting salmon to dry on the smoke rack.

He loved the way the ends of her long black hair
        brushed the surface of the water,
the way her breasts filled her "Indian Pride" tee-shirt—
        swaying from the motion of her knife;
her pink panties showing from her faded jeans.

When Birdie left to grab a soda from the ice chest,
Oscar pressed a cold salmon against his burning flesh.

Tumbleweeds

All across Eternal Poverty Indian Reservation
tumbleweeds roll across the red, arid earth:

the dry spinning husks of dreams.

So Begins the Lasting Silence

There is no doubt
I will be the last speaker
of our dying language.

I will know
that day has come
when I call out
across the frozen river
to the far white mountain
in my Native tongue
and wait forever
for an echo
that will not return—

the far white mountain
having forgotten its Indian name.

Potlatch

for Joe Secondchief

All day long guests arrive in our village
huddled along the frozen river
to mourn great uncle's death.

From the sacred circle of our clan
skin drums echo and elders sing:

'Syuu' hwtiitł nac'ełtsiin yen
A potlatch is made for him.

Pulses quicken to the rhythm
dancers stream like vibrations
across the wooden floor
heavy with rifles and blankets.

'Unggadi 'dliis kanada'yaet yen ne'et dakozet
A potlatch song is sung for him in heaven.

Tonight I have learned there is an end
to every season, to every light
where even the yawning of brittle leaves
breaks the solitude of night.

Mileposts

Graves, like mileposts,
mark the distance between our villages.

Already this summer one cousin drunk on a curve;
an old man teetering along a twisted highway;
a mislaid infant, forgotten,
gently crushed beneath the roll
of fortune's all-season tire.

As the sun wheels across a sheer sky
I stand in the heat of a great unbalanced day
watching ripples of salmon shambling upriver—
spirits of ancestors ruffling the surface
on their journey home.

In the distance, a swaggering car approaches
shining like the beautiful black steel of old guns.

How to Conquer the New World

When I was fourteen
Sanford Nicolai
spoke at a potlatch.

He looked around the Great Hall
upon many faces from different clans,
pointed out the frost-lined window

towards the far white mountains
dominating our land and myth,
spoke in the slow words of an elder,

"For over a thousand years
we call them mountains *K'ełt'aeni*.
But Indians not very smart.

Very first white man comes along,
he look up at them mountains
and say, ah, Mt. Sanford.

He write it down on a map,
and Mt. Sanford it is today,
my people."

Song of a Whale Hunter

Like a lone sentry on an edgeless world of ice
an Eskimo hunter watches for whale. Spring

has returned to the North dragging
daylight on its carved ivory sled. The

old man feels warmth return to the Arctic
as the horizon-bound sun retraces its footprints

towards summer when the lengthening days
will have no lasting darkness. He stands

witnessing the season's slow thaw and sings
a hunter's song across the sea.

When Heaven Shits on the World

In my Indian language the word
for "falling star" is *son' tsaane*
which literally means "star shit"
as if the heavens shit on the world.

Listening to the news every day
with its headlines of rapes and murders,
deceit and greed, genocide and war,
I think it could be true.

How Reservations Got Their Name

White government official comes out to see
land selected for Indian resettlement;
looks around, scratches his head and says,
"I don't know. I got some reservations about this place."

Indian Social Security

At Eternal Poverty Reservation
the First Baptist Church of Indian Conversion

bingo hall is filled with smoke and laughter,
hope and the greasy smell of fry bread,

and prayers for rent or groceries
are answered in the calling of letters and numbers.

B-32   B-32

If Willy Loman Had Been Indian

After graduating from

George Armstrong Custer High School
Simon Lone Fight got a job selling insurance
door-to-door on the reservation.

He never sold a single policy.

Other Indians just stared at him
from behind screened doors
wearing a dark suit and tie
with a briefcase and hat in his hand,
their empty hands in their empty pockets,
puzzled by his sales pitch,

wondering how one is insured against the future.

What the Tour Guide Said

"Oh, *that*," said the bus driver
in reply to a tourist's question
about a dilapidated and overgrown
white picket-fenced area just
behind the reservation's cemetery.

"That's where the failed dreams
of Indians go to be buried."

Anchorage

He said his name was Harry when a white hotdog vendor told him to stand behind the stainless steel cart where tourists wouldn't see him as they walked Fourth Avenue and into gift shops with Native souvenirs displayed in crowded storefronts. He wanted change for a dollar to call his son, but the vendor called him a drunk. "Harry, who's committing *hari kari* with booze." That's what he said, but I didn't smell anything on his breath. The Indian saw me, and while I traded coins he told me how his great grandfather was a shaman whose magic once filled Cook Inlet with shimmering salmon at a time when fish were few. He left me alone on the noisy street where two German tourists parked a zebra-striped motorcycle and ordered reindeer sausages with onions and green peppers, and a woman from New York City with a Gucci handbag passed with her catch of carved ivory and Eskimo masks.

It's All in the Blood

Herbert Redskin was in a car accident
and got a blood transfusion from a white guy.

Afterward, he burned his BIA card,
sold his allotment and moved off the rez
to a suburb where he bought a condo,
a gas grill, an SUV, golf clubs, and a flat screen TV,
wore fat-ass Dockers and polo shirts,
started a portfolio, listened to Kenny G.
and prayed at the altar of Martha Stewart.

Birthday Girl

Nila Both-Feet-on-the-Ground
came out of her mother backwards
and stood in a slick pool asking questions
about broken treaties and broken promises,
what's a reservation,
why's the house so poor;
where's her father;
why's she naked;
and why's everyone staring
at her brown and blue eyes?

Indians should always come out feet first,
ready to hit the ground and make a stand
or run at the first sign of trouble.

(Native) America Enters the Atomic Age

"Could it not be arranged to send the Small Pox among the Indians?"
—Letter from Major General Jeffery Amherst, 1763

In the spring of 1763, Chief Pontiac's second cousin
on his mother's side, Seymour Kleerlee, had a vision.

He saw an enormous silver eagle flying five miles
above the earth with the words *Enola Gay*
painted on the side. The bird laid a giant egg
that fell and exploded over a city.
In a flash as bright as the sun,
100,000 people were vaporized—
their spirits clambering into the swirling inferno.

Seymour tried to warn his people, but everyone just laughed
and said the government would never do anything so terrible.

That winter, soldiers brought them a wagonload of blankets,
and in the days and weeks to come,
death unleashed soared the earth like an eagle.

High Anxiety

Nila Both-Feet-on-the-Ground
had never flown in an airplane before.

On the first time she labeled her body parts
with a black permanent marker:

Nila's left arm, Nilas's right foot,
left breast, big toe, pinky, and so on.

During turbulence, she counted body parts
like worn beads on a rosary.

Oneupmanship

God got angry at Humanity
So he created a cataclysmic Flood.

Raven got angry at Indians
So he created Christopher Columbus.

Jimmy Stands-Too-Tall

On the day Jimmy-Stands-Too-Tall hung himself
the wind outside blew dust over everything
commercials still played on his black and white tv
his old dog spun in tight circles before lying down
the stock market was up then down and up again
traffic backed up on city freeways for miles
1,684 babies were born prematurely
Elvis was seen at a car wash
credit card companies left three messages on the phone
couples were married and divorced
children conceived and unborn
and the earth kept spinning and spinning.

But all around the world there was nothing
left of Jimmy Stands-Too-Tall
but unpaid bills, empty beer cans and bottles,
dirty dishes, and the sound of a weighted rope creaking.

Recipe for a Reztini

Two parts cheap gin or vodka
One part of your youth
Garnish with a strip of dried salmon or jerky
Shake it in the backseat of a Pontiac
doing 70 mph around Dead Man's Curve

Reservation Roulette

My cousin, Kenny, and I are sitting on the porch
of his HUD home drinking beer and bitching
about the lack of jobs.

A raven lands on a broken-down refrigerator
used to smoke salmon.
"God's come to see us," I say. We both laugh.
After six beers each, Kenny brings out his .44 magnum,

the hole so big I swear a Mack truck could turn around in it.
He loads the cylinder with one bullet,
spins it, and snaps it shut without looking.

"God wants a show," he says putting the barrel in his mouth
and pulling the trigger five times in a hurry,
like he's got some place to go.

"Shit, man!" says Kenny, grabbing another beer.
"Nothing works around here."

Ceremony

for Kenny B.

There's only so many times you can holler,
'Here, Bullet!' before one comes a runnin'.

I walk down to your grave by the river
and turn my face up to the patient sky.

In the gray shade of dusk
I see the black bird of your spirit
rising like a feather above the river
and narrow field
into a dark and rolling sundown
slowly stealing toward the blue light
of a distant pink mountain.

New Product Advertisement
from Rezlon®

Feel like a new woman with our miraculous
Indian Face Cream®

Instantly gain Wisdom, Spirituality
and Oneness with Mother Nature

Completely natural and organic
Made from the sloughed skin of genuine Indians

Indian Stompers

"August 30, 1779. Toward noon we found some dead Indians and skinned two of them from their hips down to make leather boots; one pair for Major Platt, the other for myself."
—*from the Journal of Lt. William Barton, under the command of General Sullivan's expedition against Six Nation Indians*

Good thing
it never caught on
as a fad.

Everyone
would have wanted
a pair.

Salmonomics

based on a true story

"Let me try to explain it again,"
said the man from the Department of Fish & Game
as he looked out across the divided room—

White commercial fisherman on one side;
                                                           Indians on the other.

"It's really quite simple. You Indians have always
been allowed to catch five hundred salmon
from the river each summer.
That's not going to change under our new policy.
We're only going to *increase* the number of salmon
these commercial fisherman can catch at the mouth
of the river by half a million. So, you can plainly see
that this really isn't going to impact you at all."

The commercial fishermen applauded wildly.
The Indians sat quietly doing arithmetic in their heads.

The Last Speech of
Chief Sits-on-the-Fence

after a poem by Pastor Niemöller

First they came for the Lakota
and I did not fight because I was not Lakota.

Then they came for the Sioux
and I did not fight because I was not Sioux.

Then they came for the Apache
and I did not fight because I was not Apache.

When they finally came for me
there was no one left to fight with me.

The Virginia Woolf Suicide
of Mary Caught-in-Between

Mary Caught-in-Between
must have been made of clay,

red as the soil of her ancestors.
Every time it rained

her features were dulled—
her nose and shoulders,

hips and knees, fingers and toes.
Storm after storm, she was weathered

away until one day she filled her pockets
with stones and walked into the rising river,

her feet firmly on the bottom
until she became part of its clay bed.

Dandelions in Full Bloom

On the wintry day of his execution
the Sioux poet Jimmy Blue Cloud
sang his final poem to the sun,
wrapped it tightly in sackcloth
rent from his ragged clothes
and buried it in the prison yard.

Spring after spring
the words of the poet
sprouted into dandelions,
their white fluffy heads
spreading news of his innocence
to the world.

Home

Standing on the edge of the silty river,
snowy mountains in the distance

waiting for the river to reclaim my blood,
waiting for the earth to reclaim my bones.

Red America

ignorant america, see
those Indian children
in reservation schools
failing history and english?
they will be our poets
writing the secret truths
of your guilty nation.
blind america, see
those tourist shops
full of Indian souvenirs?
they are selling our past
for trinkets made in taiwan.
selfish america, see
those Indians sleeping
on your city streets?
they are not lazy drunks
dreaming of buffalo,
they don't have jobs
because you won't hire them.
deaf america, hear
us singing at powwows?
they are not chants of
rebellion, but love songs
from a million broken hearts.
stupid america, see
that big Indian with
a knife in his hand?
he doesn't want to cut you,
he only wants to sit by a stream
in a forest and carve totems.

Tax Evasion

After being audited by the IRS seven years in a row

> Willie Armstrong bought a puppy
> named him Loophole
> paid a retired tax collector
> to beat it four times a day until it was grown.

Nowadays, that mean old dog can smell an IRS agent
a mile away, and Willie's always out the back door
and halfway across the reservation

> by the time one of them comes aknockin'.

Smoke Signal

Duke Sky Thunder on his red Indian motorcycle
at a stoplight in Albuquerque

> wearing a red bandana and a T-shirt
> that screams *Indian Pride*,
> Crazy Horse painted on the gas tank
> and a license plate that reads INJIN.

A pickup truck with two Rednecks pulls alongside.

The closer dude leans out the window and hollers,
"I hate you sonabitches!"

> The second dude with really bad teeth yells,
> "Why don't you go back wherever you came from?"

When the light turns green, Sky Thunder grins and shouts,
"Right back at ya!" and peels away—

his long black hair whipping in the wind
like a stallion's mane, the smoke signal from his tailpipe
rising like a finger.

The One-Minute Racism Test

A Black man and an Indian walk into a bar.

The Black man smiles at the White bartender and says,
"Gimme a beer, please. Whatever you got on tap."

The smiling Indian slaps a twenty on the counter and says,
"I'll take the same thing as my friend here."

For half an hour the bartender ignores their requests,
serving other customers instead.

Later, five angry White men beat them to death
in the parking lot while bystanders look on.

In this story, which person are you?

Real Live Indian

I'm sitting in a small Midwestern café when I see an old man and a boy walk up to an Indian sitting at the table next to me. "Excuse me," says the old man. "This here is my grandson." The Indian with long black hair nods hello. "What's your name?" the Indian asks the blue-eyed little boy. "My name is Timmy. I'm in the third grade." The Indian smiles, takes a bite of his pancakes. "We seen you from our table over there," says the grandfather, pointing. "And I says to Timmy . . . I says, 'that there's a real live Indian.' Darn if he didn't say, 'I didn't know there were any Indians anymore.' So I brung him over here to show him. See Timmy? A real live Indian. Go ahead, touch him. It don't rub off." Even from where I'm sitting I see the Indian's jaw clench.

My Frostbitten Heart

I remember the day it happened—
the day my heart was frozen.

Thermometer read thirty below zero when we left the cabin
to hunt caribou. Must have been minus sixty
                    with the wind chill.

Frostbit a spot above one eye. Damn thing took years
to heal. But my frozen heart never did thaw.

I've tried the usual remedies:
                  soak in a hot tub
                  sit in a sauna.

Sometimes I feel it in my chest, my frozen heart,
fragile as a snowflake, fracture lines radiating out—

ready to shatter at any minute like thin ice on a pond.

Autobiography

I try to write
the story of my life
but the words swim
backwards on the page.

So, I tear it up
toss it into the river
where the pieces turn
into a school of salmon—

the first ever
to return to the sea.

Skins

Bigshot Indianwriter tells me to stop writing about Indian stuff;
says none of the true skins will have anything to do with me.

Afterwards, Bigshot goes shopping for designer jeans
at Abercrombie & Fitch, buys polo shirts at The Gap
and a double-shot macchiato at Starbucks on his way home
to his penthouse in a Seattle skyscraper where he checks
his portfolio balance and orders Chinese take-out

while I go home to my village,
take salmon and moose meat to elders,
haul water and firewood for them,
teach Indian children how to speak Indian,
listen to Grandmother tell stories about Raven,
then help her hand out blankets at a potlatch
for a cousin who killed himself,
before I walk home in the dark
to my little cabin on the bluff above the river,
shake out my clogged dreamcatcher,
and sit looking out the window
wondering what the hell I'm supposed to write about.

The Author

John Smelcer is a tribally and federally enrolled member of Ahtna, one of the thirteen Alaska Native Corporations established by the Alaska Native Claims Settlement Act. He is a member of the Traditional Native Village of Tazlina. For three years, he was the tribally appointed executive director of the Ahtna Heritage Foundation, charged with preserving Ahtna culture, oral history, and language, and administering the annual tribal scholarship program. Taught by every living elder in his tribe, John is one of the last speakers of his severely endangered language and the only tribal member able to read and write fluently in it. In 1998, he published *The Ahtna Noun Dictionary and Pronunciation Guide* (forewords by Noam Chomsky, Ken Hale, and Steven Pinker, revised 2011). He is also one of the last speakers of Alutiiq, a neighboring, yet unrelated language, and in 2010 he edited and published a noun dictionary of that language (foreword by H. H. The Dalai Lama). In 1998, John was nominated for the Alaska Governor's Award for his contributions to the preservation of Alaska Native languages and cultures. In 2004, the Elihu Foundation of Chicago recognized John for his contributions to Native Peoples. In 2013, he was recommended to receive the Presidential Citizen's Medal for his enduring efforts to preserve America's Native heritage. John Smelcer is the author of fifty books, including his international gold medal winning short story collection *Alaskan: Stories from the Great Land*, and *Beautiful Words:*

The Complete Ahtna Poems, the only existing literature published in Ahtna. John's numerous books of poetry include *Songs from an Outcast* (UCLA's American Indian Studies Center, 2000), *Riversongs*, *The Indian Prophet*, and *Without Reservation*. His award-winning novels include *The Great Death*, *Edge of Nowhere*, *Lone Wolves*, *Savage Mountain*, and *The Trap*, which is listed among the 101 greatest novels to teach the English language. His poems appear in over 450 journals worldwide. His autobiography appears in *Here First: Autobiographical Essays by Native American Writers* (Random House, 2000). In 1994, John co-edited *Durable Breath: Contemporary Native American Poetry*. With Joseph Bruchac, he co-edited *Native American Classics* (2013), a graphic novel of 19th and early 20th century American Indian literature. John's books of Alaska Native mythology include *The Raven and the Totem* (foreword by Joseph Campbell), *A Cycle of Myths*, and *Trickster*. For a quarter century, John has served as poetry editor at *Rosebud*, making him one of the longest serving editors at a major magazine in American history. Aside from a Ph.D. in English and creative writing, John's education includes studies in poetry at Northwest Indian College and postdoctoral studies at Oxford, Cambridge, and Harvard.

Learn more at www.johnsmelcer.com